START-UP SCIENCE

Push and Pull

By Jack Challoner

Contents

Belitha Press

First published in Great Britain in 1996 by
Belitha Press Ltd

London House, Great Eastern Wharf
Parkgate Road, London SW11 4NQ

British Library Cataloguing in
Publication Data for this book
is available from the British Library.

Acknowledgements

J Allan Cash: 15
Frank Lane Photo Agency: 17 E & D Hosking, 26 G Moon.
NHPA: 7 & 8 Stephen Dalton, 18 Anthony Bannister, 30.
OSF: 23 Alan Lane.
SPL: 4 Dr Morely Read, 16 Stephen Dalton,
24 Rob Hunt, 27, 29.
Tony Stone Images: cover, 11, 13, 14, 19.
Telegraph Colour Library: 9 Jerry Young.

All other photographs by Claire Paxton.
Thanks to models Leila, Samantha, Rumman, Hasan, Tommy,
Dolly, Jacquie, Himansu, Poonam and Hardik.
Thanks to Drayton Park School.

ISBN 1-85561-506-1

Edited by Liz Harman
Series design by Hayley Cove
Designed by Helen James
Illustrated by David Gifford
Picture research by Juliet Duff and Diana Morris

Science adviser Geoff Leyland,
Head Teacher, Hady Primary School,
Chesterfield

Printed in Spain

Words in **bold** appear in the glossary on page 32.

Push and pull

This book will answer lots of questions that you may have about pushes and pulls. But it will also make you think for yourself.

Each time you turn a page, you will find an activity that you can do yourself at home or at school. You may need help from an adult.

We use pushes and pulls all the time. A push or a pull can make things move. It can also stretch, squash and even break things.

Pushing things

When we push things, they may move away from us or they may stay still. A large push is needed to move a heavy object. Not all pushes make things move.

Did you know?

Many insects are strong for their size. If this dung beetle were as big as a person, it could push a car or a lorry.

Moving soil

A new house must be built on flat ground. This bulldozer is pushing very hard to clear away the soil.

Staying still

Not all pushes make things move. This girl is pushing very hard against a house, but the house is staying where it is.

Now try this

Lighter objects are easier to move than heavier ones.

You will need
A ping pong ball, a heavy book.

1 Put the ball and the book on a table next to each other.

2 Now push each object forwards about 20 centimetres. Which do you need to push harder to move it?

Pulling things

When we pull things, they may move towards us, or they may stay still. A pull can be large or small. Can you think of any pulls?

Tug of war

These children are having a tug of war. Two teams pull in opposite directions and the team that pulls hardest will move the other team towards them.

Strong ants

Ants are very small but they can pull quite hard. This ant is moving a beetle, which is much heavier than itself.

Now try this

You can see that pulls can be big or small.

You will need
Two rubber bands, scissors, a saucer, a dinner plate, tape.

1 Ask an adult to cut the rubber bands into long strips of rubber.

2 Tape one rubber band to the saucer and the other to the plate.

3 Place the plate and saucer on the floor, and pull the ends of the rubber bands. When the plate and saucer move along the floor, which rubber band stretches the most?

Starting and stopping

A push or a pull is needed to make something move. A moving object will stop if it is pushed or pulled in the opposite direction to the way it is moving.

Leapfrog

Strong muscles in this frog's legs push hard against a leaf to launch the frog into the air.

Did you know?

You can see parking bumps in some car parks. When a car's tyres push against a bump, the bump pushes back against the tyres and helps to stop the car.

Pulled along

This aeroplane is pulling a **glider** to take it up into the air. The glider does not have an engine, so it needs to be pulled hard to start it moving.

If you push two things as hard as each other, will they both move the same distance?

You will need
A few small objects, such as toy cars, marbles or books, a ruler.

1 Put the objects in a line on a table.

2 Use the ruler to give all the objects a push at the same time. Which objects go the furthest?

Moving along

One push will not move a box very far. You need to keep pushing to keep it moving. But some things do not need a push or pull to keep them moving.

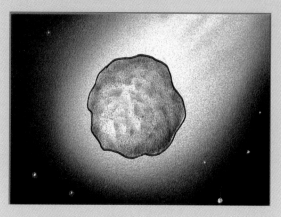

No push or pull

This girl is moving across the ground without pushing or pulling.

The wheels on her roller skates make this possible because they do not slow her down.

Pulling a plough

A plough digs up the soil on a farm. A tractor is pulling the plough to keep it moving.

Now try this

A moving object usually moves in a straight line. But a push or pull from the side can make it change direction.

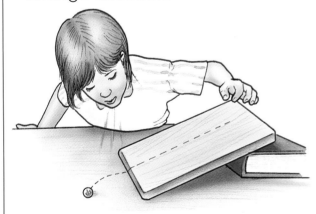

You will need
A marble, a tray.

1 Put the tray on a table. Rest one end of the tray on a book.

2 Hold the marble at the top of the tray and let go. The marble will roll along the table in a straight line.

3 Roll the marble again. This time, blow on the marble from the side. Does it still roll in a straight line?

The pull of gravity

You may have heard people talk about **gravity**. Gravity is a pull. It always pulls downwards. Gravity is invisible, so you cannot see it, but it pulls on everything.

Through the air

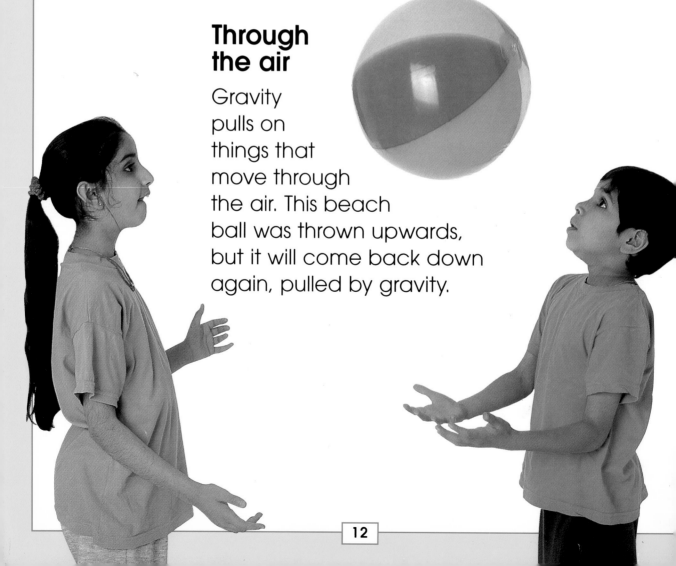

Gravity pulls on things that move through the air. This beach ball was thrown upwards, but it will come back down again, pulled by gravity.

Weighing things

Without gravity, things would weigh nothing. Gravity pulls these apples and blocks equally so they balance.

Faster and faster

Some people go sledging in the snow. Gravity pulls them down a slope, making them go faster and faster.

Now try this

Gravity pulls on heavy things more than on light things. But heavy things are harder to pull so everything falls at the same rate.

You will need
Modelling clay.

1 Make one small ball and one large ball of modelling clay.

2 Let go of both balls at the same time. They will reach the ground at the same time.

Lifting up

Gravity pulls everything downwards. The bigger something is, the stronger is the pull. To lift something, you must pull or push it upwards against gravity.

Reaching for leaves

These antelopes have strong legs, which push against the ground to lift them high enough to reach the leaves.

Tall crane

When a tall building is built, very heavy pieces have to be lifted into place. A tall crane can pull on chains which lift the object on to the building.

Now try this

You can see that heavier objects need a bigger pull to lift them than lighter ones.

You will need
Modelling clay, rubber bands, scissors.

1 Ask an adult to cut three rubber bands into long strips.

2 Make a small, a medium and a large lump of clay.

3 Push one end of a rubber band into each lump and lift the other end. Which lump stretches the rubber the most?

Stretching and squashing

Sometimes, a pull or a push can stretch or squash an object. The harder the pull or push, the more the object will stretch or squash, changing its shape.

Hitting a ball

A golfer has just hit this ball with a golf club. Can you see where the golf ball has changed shape as a result of being hit?

Did you know?

Earthworms have no legs. They stretch and squash their bodies to move along.

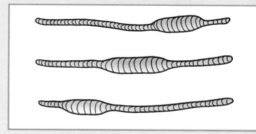

Stretchy beak

This pelican is holding a meal of fish in its **bill**. Gravity pulls the fish down so the weight of the fish pulls on the bird's bill, stretching it.

Now try this

The harder you push something, the more it squashes.

You will need
A rubber ball.

1 Hold the ball between your hands.

2 Push gently at first, then harder. When does the ball squash the most?

Bending and breaking

Sometimes, a pull or a push will bend an object. A very hard pull or push can even break an object.

Hatching out

Baby snakes like this one hatch out of eggs. When it is ready to hatch, the baby snake pushes hard enough to break the shell.

Bendy pole

This bendy pole sends the pole vaulter high into the air as it straightens.

Now try this

When you bend something, one side of it squashes and the other side stretches.

You will need
A long rubber.

1 Hold the rubber between a finger and thumb.

2 Push your fingers together so that the rubber bends.

3 Look closely at the rubber. Which side has squashed and which side has stretched?

Twisting and turning

A push or a pull can twist an object or start it turning. The harder the push or the pull, the more the object twists or the faster it turns.

When tennis players hit a ball, they often make it spin by pushing the ball with their tennis racket when they hit it.

Winding up

This model plane has a **propeller**. A twisted rubber band turns the propeller as it unwinds. This boy is pushing the propeller to twist the rubber band.

On the roundabout

To make a roundabout turn, someone needs to push quite hard.

Now try this

You can make a spinner which will turn round very fast if you twist it with your fingers.

You will need
A short crayon, thin card.

1 Cut the card into a square about 5 by 5 centimetres.

2 Ask an adult to push the crayon through the middle of the card.

3 Twist the crayon to spin the card. Colour your spinner and then see what happens when you spin it.

The push of water

If you were a diver at the bottom of the sea, the water around you would push on your body. Water pushes in all directions and can push through holes.

Squirting water

Water can push itself through holes and squirt out. Is the push of the water hardest at the top or at the bottom of this bottle?

Did you know?

The push of water can make things turn round. Water wheels like this used to power machines in factories.

Holding back water

This beaver has built a strong **dam**, which holds back the push of water in a river, making a small lake.

Now try this

See for yourself that water pushes in all directions. Make sure you do this outside.

You will need
Water, a balloon, a towel, sticky tape, a pin.

1 Ask an adult to fill the balloon half full with water, and to tie the balloon at the neck.

2 Dry the balloon, and stick pieces of tape firmly to it in three different places.

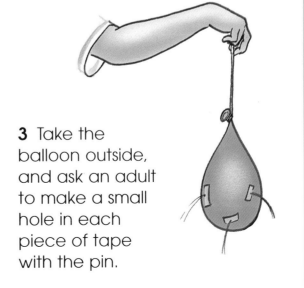

3 Take the balloon outside, and ask an adult to make a small hole in each piece of tape with the pin.

The push of air

Just as water pushes, so does air. Although you cannot feel it, the air around you is pushing on you right now.

Riding on air

Did you know?

When you suck the air out of a drinking straw, the air around the drink pushes the drink up the straw and into your mouth.

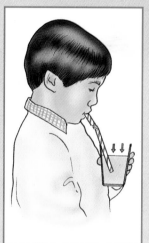

This hovercraft is on dry land. When it travels over water it is lifted off the surface of the water by air. Large fans squash the air underneath the hovercraft.

Pumping up a tyre

This girl is pumping air into her bicycle tyre. The more air she pumps in, the more the air inside pushes, making the tyres feel very firm.

Now try this

You can see how squashed air pushes harder than ordinary air.

You will need
A bicycle pump.

1 Hold the hole in the pump firmly against a finger.

2 Now, pull out the pump handle, and gently push it in again. Can you feel the air pushing back as it is squashed?

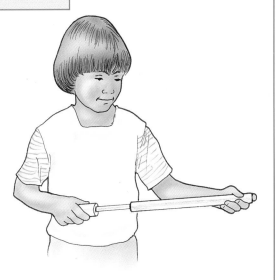

Moving air

Air is all around you. Outside, air moves around. Moving air is called wind. The wind can push on things. The faster the wind blows, the harder it pushes.

Sailing boat

Can you see how the wind fills the sails with air as it pushes these boats along?

When there is no wind, the boats will not move through the water.

Strong wind

During a storm, the wind often blows very fast. When it blows fast, it pushes hard. Very strong winds can damage houses.

Now try this

You can see how fast air is moving by seeing how much it pushes.

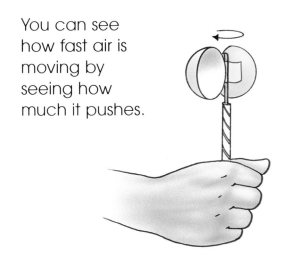

You will need
A ping pong ball, a drinking straw, a wooden skewer, tape.

1 Ask an adult to cut the ping pong ball in half and tape the halves to the top of the skewer.

2 Push the skewer into the straw. Go outside and hold the straw. The balls will turn around faster in a strong wind.

Magnets and electricity

Have you ever used a **magnet**? Magnets can pull metal objects, and can pull and push other magnets. **Static electricity** can also pull and push.

Electricity pulling

This balloon has been rubbed against a woollen jumper. It is pulling the boy's hair towards it. This is called static electricity.

Did you know?

If two balloons are rubbed on a woollen jumper, they will push apart when held close to each other.

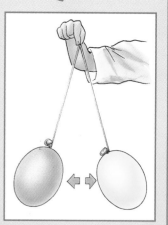

Magnetic train

There is a huge magnet on the bottom of this train, and more magnets on the track beneath it. The two magnets push apart, lifting the train into the air.

Now try this

Magnets can pull and push other magnets.

You will need
Two magnets.

1 Hold the magnets near to each other.

2 Can you make the magnets pull each other and push each other away?

Plants and animals

Many animals push and pull. Stronger animals push and pull harder than others.

Plants push their roots deep under the ground, in search of water.

Climbing a tree

To lift itself up a tree, this monkey is pulling hard on the tree's bark. The heavier the monkey is, the harder it must push upwards.

Did you know?

A fish bends its body so that it can push against the water. This is how it moves along in the water.

Strong roots

The strong roots of this tree have pushed their way through the ground. They have even pushed up the hard surface of the path.

Now try this

You can see for yourself how the roots of a plant push down, looking for water.

You will need
A broad bean seed, an empty jar, kitchen paper.

1 Put the kitchen paper round the inside of the jar.

2 Put the bean seed between the paper and the glass. Put some water in the jar.

3 Look at the seed every day. After a few days, a root and a shoot will grow from the seed.

Glossary

bill The beak of a bird.

dam A barrier which blocks a river or stream, making a lake or pool.

glider An aircraft which has no engine and glides through the air.

gravity A force that pulls objects towards the Earth.

magnet A piece of metal which pulls other magnets or iron towards it. Two magnets can also push apart.

propeller A type of flat paddle which spins round and propels (pushes) an aircraft through the air or a boat through water.

static electricity An electrical force which can pull objects towards it.

tornado A very strong wind which spins around in a circle and can pull large objects into its centre.

Index